ISBN: 0-9895735-6-7
ISBN-13: 978-0-9895735-6-6

Library of Congress Control No.: 2017912243

Published by: studioWorks

I0025396

For: *the children of Trinity Preschool of Berwyn, whose joyful spirit inspires and amazes me every day, and for the staff and families whose support and encouragement make the day possible.*

donna

For: *my alma mater, the wonderful Trinity Preschool, and for the Conestoga Studio Art program which helped me develop my artistic capabilities.*

alice

CONTENTS

INTRODUCTION

Focusing a preschool class on *growing things* makes inherent sense, since young children are fascinated by exactly how old they are, when their next birthday is, how tall they are, and much they've grown – since yesterday.

Extending this interest was simple and easily engaged them in learning. But I needed a book with which to begin the class, one that explored the concept of how everything is growing; from children to the natural world and all the way to our planet and the universe. So I decided to write that book, and recruited a partner to collaborate with me through illustrations.

Too far or too much for preschoolers to understand? Not at all, especially when the learning starts with things with which they are already familiar; themselves, flowers, animals, trees. They are also captivated by dramatic and exciting things like volcanoes and outer space, so this book easily stretches them to think about a basic concept (growth) in a different way. The common theme of growing also facilitates learning that everything in life is related, while introducing what for them may be novel concepts; that the Earth is a dynamic, growing planet and that our universe is expanding.

We are growing, oh, so fast
Getting bigger – stronger, too
Having fun along the way
Watching, learning how to do

Animals are growing too
Babies born so vulnerably
Quickly learn to run, fly, swim
On their own they soon will be

Once small seeds, trees are growing
Adding rings with sights set high
Rooted firmly in the ground
Branches reach up to the sky

Everywhere plants are growing
In the proper spot, they will
Desert, jungle, ocean, woods
Garden, farm, or windowsill!

Bit by bit, all mountains grow
Pushing up from deep below
Pinnacles now tower above
Where once plateaus lay long ago

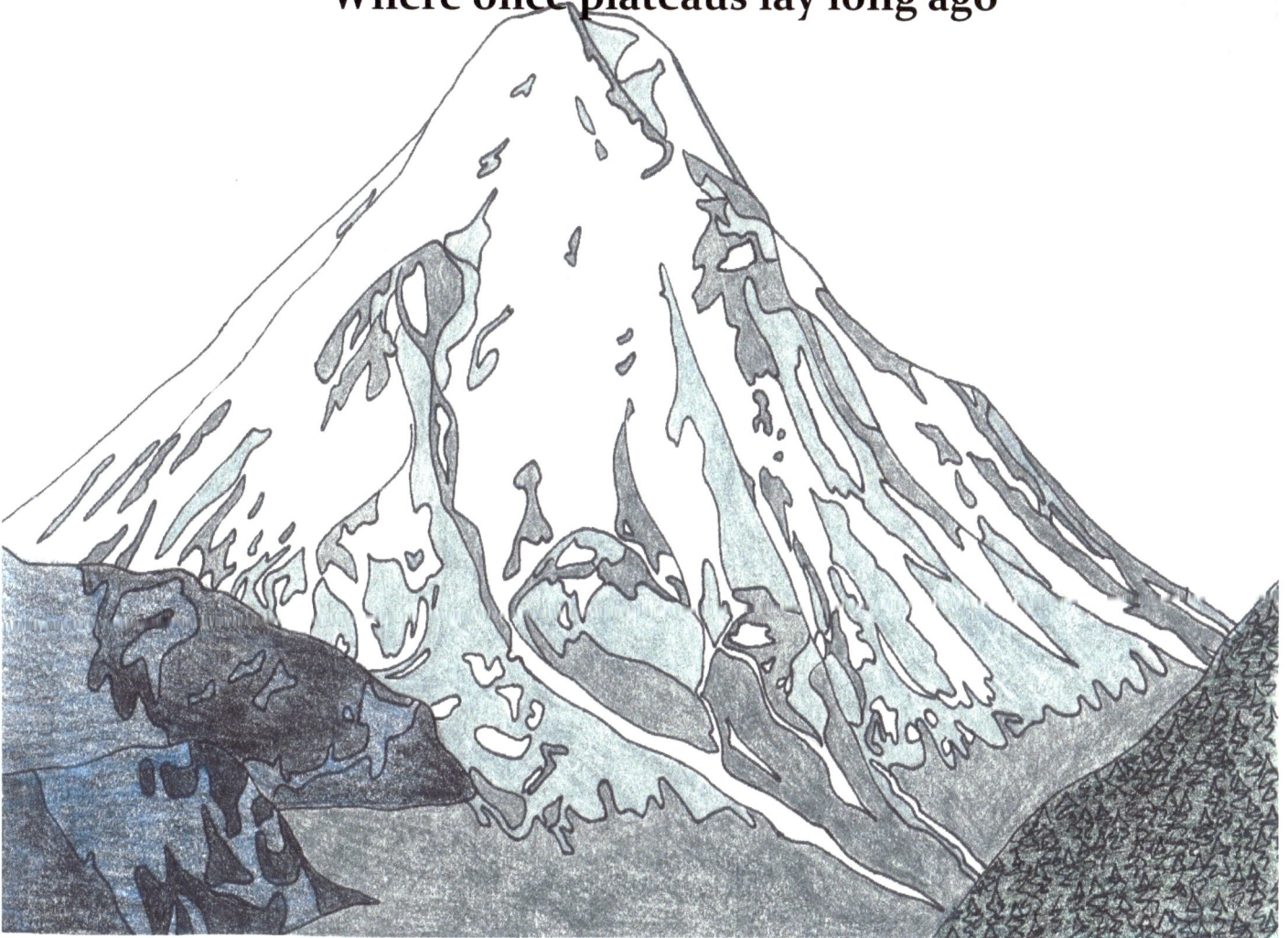

**Underneath, Earth is growing
Its molten hot magma core
Shoots lava up from the sea
Brand new land forms with a roar**

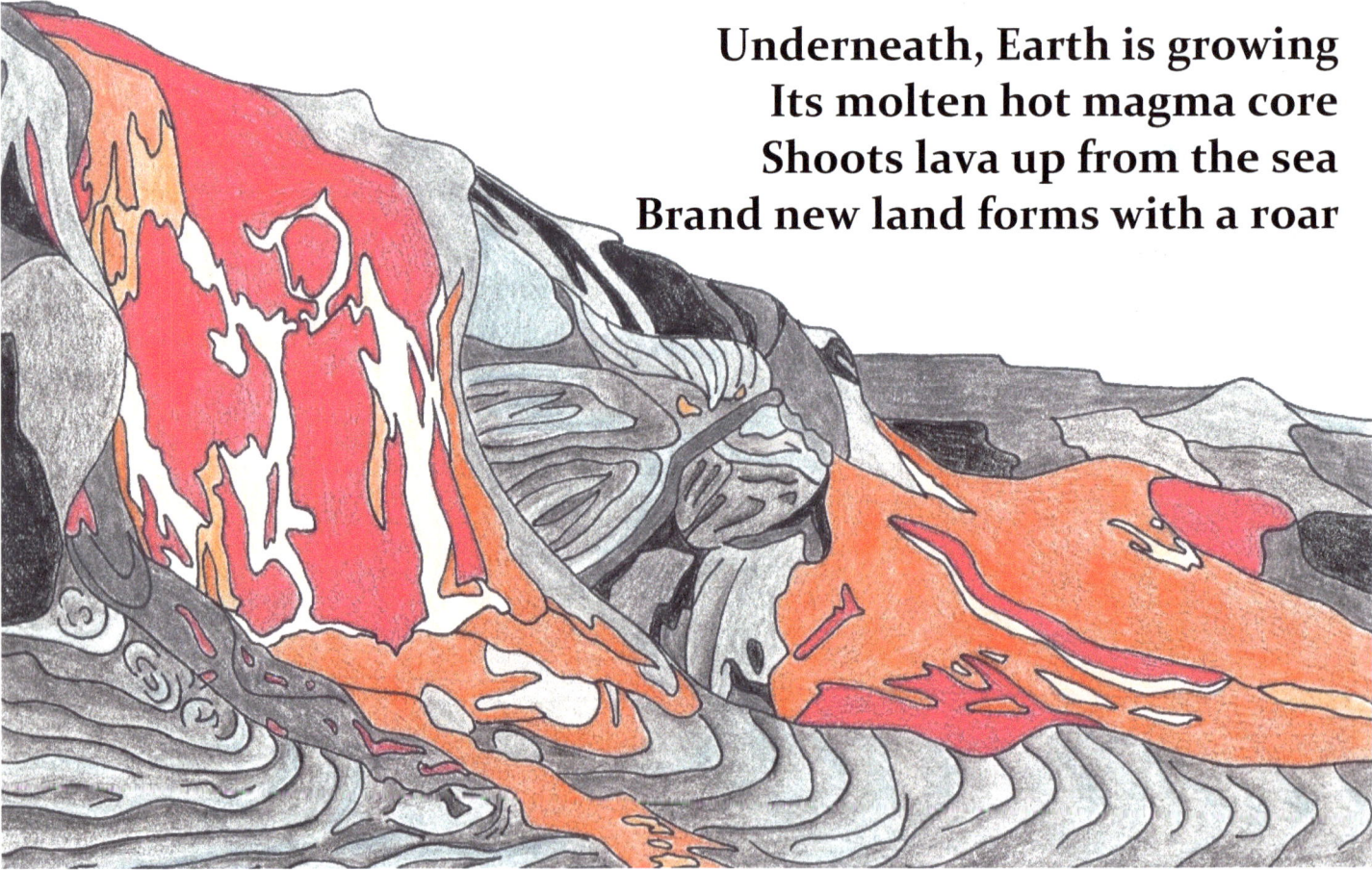

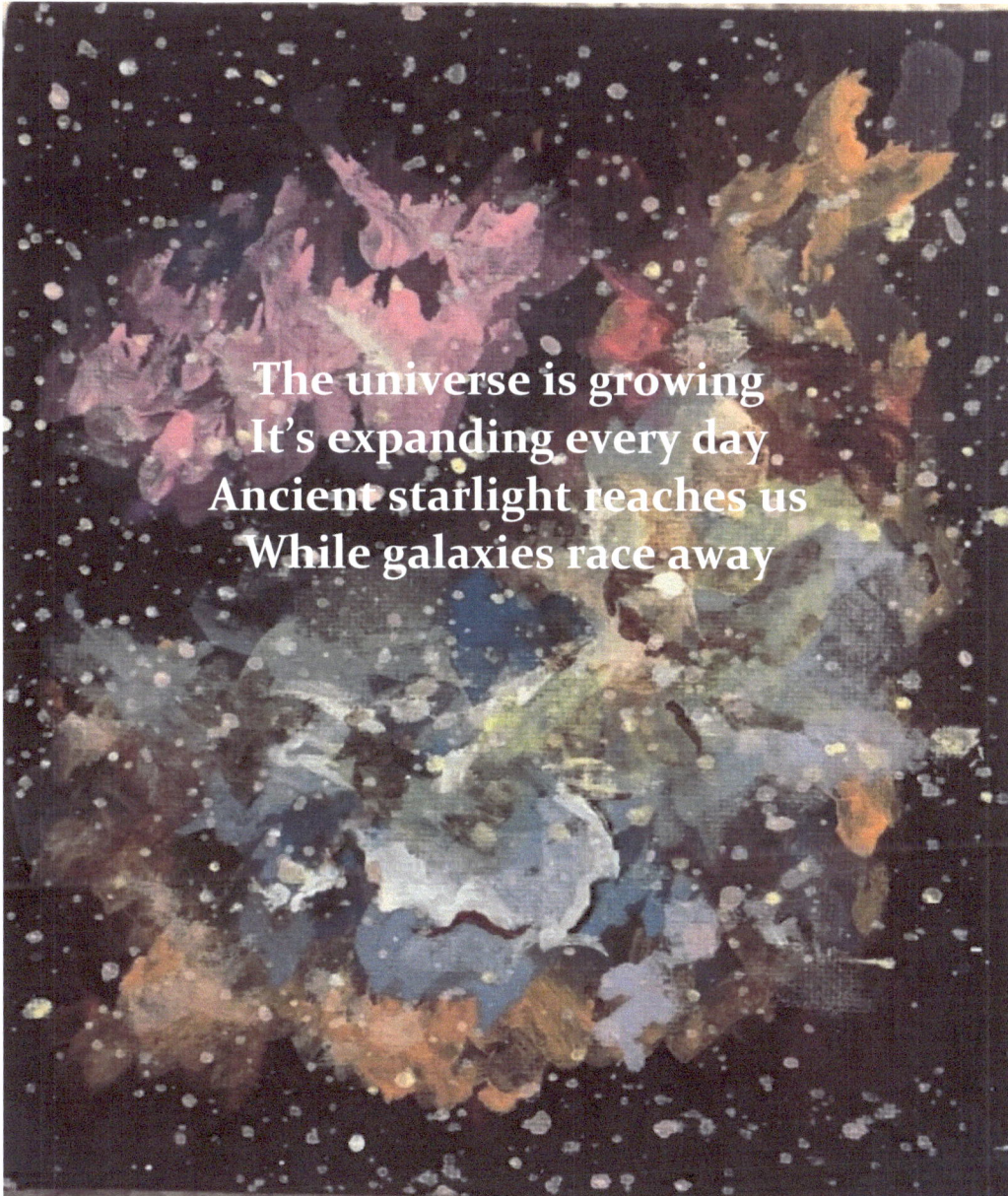

The universe is growing
It's expanding every day
Ancient starlight reaches us
While galaxies race away

Glossary

This book purposely includes words that children might not know, providing an opportunity to learn new, fun vocabulary. Being able to express yourself is an important skill, critical for literacy, and a great joy! Here are some of the words from the story and their definitions.

Vulnerable: open to easy attack, harm, and danger and requiring extra care and protection to be kept safe.

Tree Rings: Trees mark their growth by annually adding another ring of cellulose (that's the main part of what plants, including trees, are made). These rings are not equal in size. Their width depends on how well the tree grew that year: if a tree received lots of water, nutrients, and the right amount of light, it will lay down a wider ring than in a year of drought, for example. When a tree is cut down, the rings can be counted to find out how old it is. Scientists use tree ring records to find out information about the past, such as what the climate was like in a particular year.

Desert: Land that does not receive much rain or snow, and usually has mostly sand, rock, and little soil. The climate in a desert tends to be quite hot during the day and yet very cold at night. Only certain plants and animals are able to live there, those that have adapted to such harsh conditions.

Jungle: Land that gets a lot of rain resulting in an abundance of plants and wide diversity of animal life. Usually located in tropical areas or temperate climates, jungles can be found in many places around the world. The climate in a jungle tends to be hot and steamy, or warm and misty.

Forest: Land mainly covered by trees, with bushes and smaller plants growing underneath (known as undergrowth); shelters a variety of animal life. The type of trees, plants, and animals found in a forest depend on the location of the forest (northern boreal, coastal, mountainous, temperate, etc.)

Ocean: Refers to the huge body of salt water that covers ¾ of Earth and ranges from polar to tropical and everything in between. The ocean harbours diverse plant and animal life that varies greatly depending on the region and the depth. The ocean starts at beachside and gets as deep as 10,994 meters in the Mariana Trench in the Pacific Ocean — possibly deeper!

Pinnacle: The highest peak, or the very top, of a mountain or hill.

Plateau: Level, flat land that is higher than the surrounding area, sometimes with a steep drop on one or more sides and/or a canyon running through. Also may be called a high plain or tableland.

Magma: Hot fluid or semifluid material under Earth's surface: it can cool and form rocks both underneath Earth and after flowing out onto Earth's surface as lava.

Lava: Molten rock that flows from a volcano or crack in Earth's surface and hardens into rock as it cools.

Molten: A melted or liquid state of material caused by heat.

Star: Bright, shining spheres of plasma that gravity holds together. Earth's closest star is the sun. The night sky (especially when observed away from cities and other sources of light) is aglow with many other more distant stars (some so far away that their light is just now reaching us even though they burned out long ago).

Sphere: Round ball shaped object.

Plasma: Gas that has an equal amount of positive and negative particles, so it has no electrical charge – it's a balanced gas, so to speak.

Universe: All of the planets, stars, galaxies, matter, energy, space, and time that exists (all that ever has existed and will exist, so pretty much the total of everything ever).

Galaxy: A collection of planets, stars, gas, and dark matter that is bound together by gravity and separated from other galaxies by a lot of space; galaxies tend to cluster and group together throughout the universe, and there might be over 100 billion in the universe. If you can't get to sleep, instead of counting sheep perhaps try counting galaxies. If that doesn't work, try coming up with names for all of them.

Gravity: A force of nature that causes objects with mass to draw together, from atoms, to us not floating away from Earth's surface, to planets orbiting the sun.

***Wait, expanding universe? Yes, that's what research shows....but that's another book. Involving astrophysics. Possibly quantum mechanics. Look at how a project grows.......

About the Author

Since preschool didn't exist way back when and where Donna was young and living in the mountains of Swaziland, she instead followed her own curriculum of running around the hills, climbing trees, scolding the goats to get out of the garden (in multiple languages since it's still unclear to which language goats best respond), fleeing from escapee chickens, building in the dirt with friends, pretending to call her grandparents in Toronto, practicing proper afternoon tea protocol, and teaching herself to read.

Don't worry, she was guarded by her corgi, Vipi. Oh, plus supervision was provided by her parents and Nkhososama Ruth, who kept track of her via bells on her shoes. A huge thank you to them. May every child have the safety and freedom to explore childhood and outdoors in such a way.

Much later on, she earned her Master's degree, in part by studying how children learn vocabulary and to tell stories. Donna founded studioWorks Publishing to provide books that spark curiosity, inspire adventure, exploration, and learning about nature and science, discovering the world, and capturing the innate wonder of childhood...for all ages.

@studioworks_pub

www.studioworkspublishing.blogspot.com

About the Illustrator

Alice grew up in Berwyn, Pennsylvania, sandwiched between two brothers.

She got her start at Trinity Preschool of Berwyn where she spent as much time as she could racing on the swing set.

She later discovered her love of art at Beaumont Elementary, and continued to explore art through the programs offered by the Tredyffrin- Easttown School District.

She is now a student at Pennsylvania State University, studying Psychology and Business.

Growth Chart

How Tall Are You? How Much Have You Grown? Let's Take a Look!

Birth   _____

6 Months   _____

1 Year   _____

2 Years   _____

3 Years   _____

4 Years   _____

5 Years   _____

6 Years   _____

*If this book has been borrowed from a library, please make a copy of the activity pages instead of writing on the pages. Thank you!

How Big Will You Be?

How Tall Are You Now? How Tall Do You Think You'll Grow?

Write down your height, and draw a picture of yourself. Then write down what you think your height will be when you're grown up and what you think you'll look like!

What Have You Learned?

What can you do now that you couldn't when you were younger?
Write a list or draw pictures!

*If this book has been borrowed from a library, please make a copy of the activity pages instead of writing on the pages. Thank you!

What Do You Want to Learn?

What do you want to learn how to do? What do you want to learn about?
Write a list or draw pictures!

*If this book has been borrowed from a library, please make a copy of the activity pages instead of writing on the pages. Thank you!

More Fun!

Here's some other activities based on exploring things that grow. For details see the series of "The Books We Read and the Things We Did" at:
www.studioworkspublishing.blogspot.com

Many plants cannot grow without pollinators such as bees and butterflies.

Learning about different types of seeds by making collages.

Pinecone bird feeders help birds survive the cold winter.

Adding compost so the soil has nutrients to grow plants for food.

Activities

Toad Abodes: shelter for garden toads from summer heat and winter cold.

Transplanting beans grown in clear cups to observe their growth.

Building bird feeders; important because plants that feed birds don't grow in winter.

Observing gradual growth of crystals from mineral solutions.

Activities

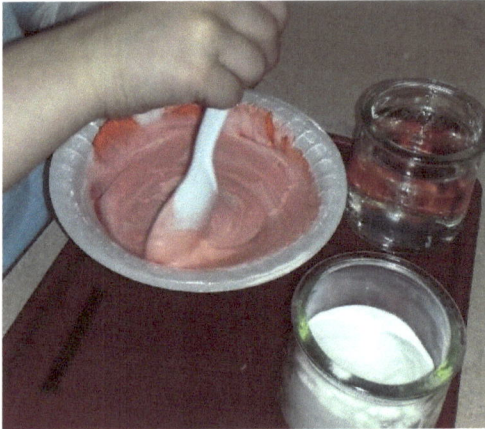

Preparing saline slime with baking soda to make a volcano.

Adding vinegar makes the volcano "erupt"!

Nebulae, stars, planets, and rocket ships are part of a space exploration bin.

www.ingramcontent.com/pod-product-compliance
Lightning Source LLC
Chambersburg PA
CBHW060856270326
41934CB00002B/156